SEEKING JUSTICE

The Madeleine McCann
And Julia Wandelt Story

FAITH HOPE JUSTICE

Copyright © 2025

All rights reserved

All scripture quotations are from the
King James Version (KJV) Holy Bible

ISBN: 9798312641998

Content Warning: This book contains information on topics that might be sensitive to certain readers. Reader discretion is advised.

DEDICATION

This book is dedicated to Julia Wandelt.

She has worked so hard to compile and present the evidence she needed to support her belief. All she ever wanted was a simple DNA test that would allow her to know her true identity.

John 8:32
And ye shall know the truth, and the truth shall make you free.

Table of Contents

A Brief Introduction 7

Who is Madeleine McCann? 13

Who is Julia Wandelt? 17
    What are her memories? 26
    Who should have helped her? 33
    The Operation Grange Phone Call 34
    List of Prescribed Medications 44

The Cover Up Culture 49
    Who are they protecting? 55

Who is telling the truth? 64

Final Conclusion 76

Uplifting Bible Verses 82

A Brief Introduction

Proverbs 29:26; *Many seek the ruler's favour; but every man's judgment cometh from the Lord.*

For various reasons, I decided to write this book under the pseudonym of; Faith Hope Justice. As one of Julia's supporters, I want to help to spread awareness of her story. It's absolutely unbelievable, how badly she has been treated, even by authorities who should have helped her. The lack of support, and rejection that she continues to receive, has prevented her from being able to prove, or disprove, who she really is.

The Madeleine McCann case is a matter of public interest, and considering that over thirteen million pounds of public money has already been spent on the case, it's about time that we got some answers. As far as the public are aware, this is an open investigation, and the search for Madeleine McCann is still ongoing.

Although there are many people who believe that Madeleine is dead, there is no concrete evidence to support that theory. As a result, Madeleine should be presumed to be alive, rather than presumed to be dead. If the police have sufficient evidence to prove that Madeleine is no longer alive, then they need to share this information with the public. Either, this is a murder investigation, or it's a missing person investigation. It's one or the other, and the public have the right to know the truth!

Seeking Justice

By the end of the 2024 to 2025 financial year, Operation Grange were still receiving public funding for the case. Therefore, there is no excuse for the police not to do everything they can, whilst searching for Madeleine McCann. The public expects that all lines of enquiries, plus any potential leads, would be properly followed up, pursued, and investigated.

If someone matching the description of Madeleine McCann, were to contact the police, reporting that they could be a British missing child, it goes without saying, that the police would be expected to investigate their claim. In this type of scenario, it's pretty obvious that the missing child would have grown up under a different name, and most likely a different date of birth too.

This means the only way to establish their true identity, would be to conduct a DNA test. DNA tests are inexpensive, and extremely reliable, but in 2022 when Julia Wandelt first contacted Operation Grange, her concerns were dismissed and without doing any kind of testing, Julia was told outright, that she is not Madeleine McCann.

Without doing an official DNA test on Julia, or her parents, Operation Grange cannot say with certainty that Julia Wandelt is not Madeleine McCann. Some believe it's because the police know that Madeleine is dead, but what if it's much deeper and darker than that? I know it's hard to comprehend, but what if Operation Grange have known all along, where, and who, the real

Seeking Justice

Madeleine McCann is?

I have listened to Julia's account, and saw the evidence that she gathered, and in my opinion, I strongly believe that Julia Wandelt, is in fact Madeleine McCann. Those who have heard Julia's side of the story, will understand why Operation Grange, or other individuals, may want to cover up the truth.

If Julia's is telling the truth, then not only was she a victim of child sex-trafficking, but she would also be able to expose some of the inconceivable acts that have been carried out by certain individuals who may be well-respected by the public. Although some celebrities have already been exposed for their inappropriate behaviours, unfortunately there are many more who haven't.

Since 2022, Julia has reached out to various missing persons organisations, as well as several police forces, to report her belief, that she may be a British citizen who was kidnapped as a child. Despite the importance of her allegations, it is evident that the expected actions have not been carried out, and that her claims have not been properly investigated.

If anyone suggests that they might have been kidnapped as a child, if their alleged parents are still alive, those parents should be obligated by law, to do a DNA test, to prove that they are the child's biological parents. Documents such as birth certificates, can easily be forged, and even if they are legitimate and genuine documents, there is always the potential that those documents may have originally been issued for another individual.

There have been several child kidnappings in the past, where parents have been known to replace a deceased child, with a kidnapped child. Despite these risks, Julia's allegations were dismissed without any kind of investigation.

Operation Grange has failed to provide Julia with any evidence to support their claim, so it's no surprise that Julia would struggle to accept their opinion as being true. For some reason, Julia's search for answers about her identity, has consistently been dismissed. When Julia decided to go public with her claim in 2023, the media were extremely quick to shut her down, and portray her in a negative way.

Although it is common for the mainstream media to mix truth with lies, in Julia's case, some of the lies seem to have been used as a way of intentionally discrediting and tarnishing her credibility. The unfair rejection that Julia had to face, prior to her going public, makes me believe there could have been some sort of conspiracy against her.

Since the very beginning of this case, the McCann parents have insisted that they are a victim in all of this. They proclaim they will do anything to find their long-lost daughter, but when Julia requested a DNA test with them, they refused. If they are supposed to be searching for their missing daughter, then their actions are highly questionable.

Seeking Justice

Although Kate McCann is an ambassador for a charity that supports missing people, she seems to have no interest in helping Julia find out who she is. Julia has made several attempts to contact the McCann family, but instead of agreeing to a DNA test, the McCann family have made themselves become the victim in this situation, and have decided to report Julia to the police for harassment.

Based on their complaint, on Wednesday, February 19, 2025, Julia was arrested in the UK when she landed at Bristol Airport. She was kept in custody, and on Friday, February 21, Julia was officially charged for allegedly Stalking and Harassing the McCann family. Unfortunately, Julia has been remanded in custody until her next court hearing, which should take place on April 22, 2025.

The treatment that Julia has received is far from normal. It seems as though someone is trying to silence her, by preventing her from speaking her truth. In a strange turn of events, and only days before her arrest, Julia was advised to temporarily remove all of her social media posts. Maybe it was just a coincidence that she was arrested during that time, but timing wise, it all seems very strange.

Due to the removal of her posts, nearly all of Julia's evidence is no longer available online. Nevertheless, through various sources, I have put together much of the information that she had previously shared, so that her story is not lost, and her voice is not silenced.

Seeking Justice

In this book I am Seeking Justice for Julia Wandelt, as well as for Madeleine McCann. Julia has been seeking answers about her true identity since 2022, and she deserves to know who she really is. I hope that the information included within this book will help you to decide who is telling the truth.

Romans 8:28; *And we know that all things work together for good to them that love God, to them who are the called according to his purpose.*

Below is a quotation from one of Julia's previous social media posts:

"I sacrificed everything for the truth and justice, and my basic human's rights were totally broken by the police and law institutions, and all these people who should be here for me and other children. They didn't do their job. They just don't care. I lost everything, and I lost everyone, because of trying to get the truth and justice, and I don't know what else I can do. I don't know!"

Who is Madeleine McCann?

Matthew 18:6; *But whoso shall offend one of these little ones which believe in me, it were better for him that a millstone were hanged about his neck, and that he were drowned in the depth of the sea.*

Madeleine McCann was born in Leicester, England on May 12, 2003. Her parents Kate McCann, and Gerry McCann met in 1993, and married in 1998. It has been said that Madeleine was conceived through IVF treatment, after her parents had been trying to conceive for five years. Her twin siblings, Sean and Amelie, were also conceived through IVF, and were born on February 1, 2005.

On Saturday, April 28, 2007, the McCann family, along with some of their friends, left England for a seven-night family vacation in Lagos, which is located in the Algarve region of Portugal. The family stayed in Praia da Luz, at the Ocean Club Resort. The specific apartment that the McCann family had, was apartment 5A, and it was located on the ground floor.

Although the apartment could be accessed by the public, the McCanns have confirmed, that on more than one occasion the children were left alone in the apartment. Throughout the holiday, the children were routinely left alone in the apartment during the evening hours, whilst the rest of the adult group dined at the

Seeking Justice

Tapas Restaurant, approximately 100 yards away.

According to an account given by Kate, on the morning of Thursday, May 3, 2007, Madeleine asked her mum, why she didn't come to her during the night, when her and her brother were crying. Despite the fact that her children had been upset and crying in the apartment the night before, Kate and Gerry felt that it was still appropriate for them to leave their three-year-old daughter, and two-year-old twins, alone and in an unlocked, foreign apartment.

Later that night, around 8:30pm, after putting the children to bed, the McCanns left the apartment and went to the Tapas Restaurant. Apparently, the children were checked on every 30 minutes. At 10:00pm, when it was Kates turn to check on the children, that is when she is said to have discovered that Madeleine was gone. The police were informed, and the suggestion from Kate, was that Madeleine had been taken.

Twelve days later, on Tuesday, May 15, 2007, the Portuguese police were searching the home of their first suspect, Robert Murat. This was the same day that the McCanns decided to officially register and incorporate a new business, which they called; Madeleines Fund: Leaving No Stone Unturned.

Nothing was found to prove Murat's involvement, and there were no real developments about where Madeleine was. Due to many inconsistencies with the accounts that were given, the Portuguese police felt that they were unable to produce a reconstruction of the events. By September 7, 2007, the Portuguese police declared that they were now treating Kate and Gerry as suspects in their daughter's disappearance.

Kate and Gerry were still allowed to travel, and two days later, on September 9, 2007, Kate and Gerry returned to the UK. Unfortunately, as there were no developments in the case, on July 21, 2008, the case was archived, and the investigations of the Portuguese police came to a close. As a result, Kate and Gerry, along with Robert Murat, were no longer considered suspects in the case.

On Madeleine's 8th birthday, May 12, 2011, the Metropolitan Police announced that the Home Office would fund a specialist unit called, Operation Grange, to carry out an investigative review on all of the investigations so far in the Madeleine McCann case. This was also the same date, that Kate released her version of events in her book, titled; "Madeline: Our daughter's disappearance and the continuing search for her."

By June 2020, the German police were investigating a suspect, known as Christian B, and in April 2022, he was officially declared as being the prime suspect in the Madeleine McCann case. The police now considered this to be a murder investigation, and in May 2023, they carried out further searches in Portugal. However, nothing relevant was found, and although Christian B is still believed to be the prime suspect, he has not been convicted with any offences in relation to the Madeleine McCann case.

Seeking Justice

Although there are many theories out there, that leads some to believe that Madeleine McCann is dead, it is important to remember that there is no concrete evidence to support this theory. The fact remains that this is an open investigation for the search of Madeleine McCann, who is a missing British citizen. It is still very possible for Madeleine to be alive and well, but living under a false identity.

Jeremiah 31:17; *And there is hope in thine end, saith the Lord, that thy children shall come again to their own border.*

Who is Julia Wandelt?

Psalms 91:1; *He that dwelleth in the secret place of the most High shall abide under the shadow of the Almighty.*

According to her birth certificate, Julia Wandelt was born in August 2001, which would make her two years older than Madeleine McCann. However, just because Julia has a birth certificate, that does not prove her true identity. Children can often be big or small for their age, so if Madeleine was slightly big for her age, then it would not be unusual for her to have been given a new identity with an older age.

According to an article written in the Daily Mail, on February 23, 2025, by Nick Pisa, when Julia's parents separated, her father moved to Germany, and Julia moved to Wroclaw with her mother Dorota Wandelt-Cholewinski, and her stepfather Piotr Cholewinski. Piotr works in finance, and Dorota is a successful businesswoman who runs a chain of children clothes shops, under the name Coccodrillo. Together they were able to provide Julia with a private school education.

The article also says that a former school friend said that Julia was 'around seven years old', when she moved to Wroclaw, and joined the private school. If Julia was seven years old, then this would have occurred in 2008, only one year after Madeleine was abducted. At that time, Madeleine would have then been five years old.

Seeking Justice

According to a list that was published in The Sun, on April 30, 2017, of possible Madeleine McCann sightings, the list was also republished on July 28, 2020, number 76 on the list, was of a sighting that occurred in Wroclaw, Poland, on May 12, 2007, by a medical student. This was only nine days after Madeleine was abducted, and the medical student believed they had seen a child similar to Madeleine, accompanied by a tough looking man, in a taxi.

Although Julia is said to have attended a private school, for some reason, she was not able to settle down, and was later moved to a public school. Julia can't account for how she learnt English, but I believe she said that she was told by one of her school teachers, that when she joined the school, she already knew how to speak English.

Around 2009, when Madeleine would have been six years old, and Julia would have been eight years old, Julia is believed to have had some kind of fracture, or brain injury, where she temporarily lost the ability to walk, and talk.

When Julia was, somewhere around the age of nine years old, she was abused by her step grand-father, Peter Ney. Julia told her mother about the abuse, but her mother didn't report it to the police, and instead she allowed Peter Ney to continue having contact with Julia. I believe it was the school who later informed the police. The matter went to court, and Peter Ney was tried, and found guilty of the offence, and sentenced to some time in prison.

Seeking Justice

From the age of nine, Julia was required to take tablets on a daily basis. The medication given was not suitable for children, as confusion and memory loss, were commonly listed as a potential side effect for those medications. She was prescribed these medications for five years. Julia suffered with recurring nose bleeds, and has severe bone pain throughout her body, so it is very possible that the medication she was given, could have affected her health in multiple ways.

In her teenage years, Julia participated in some professional photo shoots, and was even selected for a Vogue magazine shoot. Julia loves to sing, and is also very gifted in music. She can play the guitar, and the piano, and has written a few original songs of her own.

During high school, Julia learnt that it would be very unlikely for a child to have blue or green eyes, if their parents both had brown eyes. Although Julia found the information slightly confusing, at that time, she did not suspect that her parents, would not have been her real parents, so she didn't really dwell on the information.

Over time, as Julia continued to struggle with the effects of being abused as a child, as well as the gaps in her memories, on more than one occasion she tried to commit suicide. In 2018, when she was 16 years old, she was hospitalised after one of those attempts. It was also after one of those attempts, that Julia asked her mother for therapy, to which she agreed.

Whilst Julia was having therapy, she started to ask

her mother a lot of questions. Due to the types of questions that Julia was now asking, her mother decided to stop the therapy, somewhere around February 2021. Her mother believed the therapy was not helping the situation, and said it was causing more problems.

Julia often felt a level of disconnect from her mother, and could not understand why her mother allowed her to continue seeing Peter Ney, even after she had been told about the abuse. Julia asked her mother whether or not she was adopted, but her mother insisted that she gave birth to Julia, and that she was not adopted.

Due to Julia's doubts and concerns, she also sought answers from her father. Although he insisted that he was her father, on one occasion, in response to her question, Julia said he asked her whether it would change anything, even if he wasn't. Julia also asked her father, whether or not Peter Ney had any other victims. This was when her father disclosed that Peter Ney had previously been involved in kidnappings. This led Julia to believe that she could actually be a kidnapped child.

After this, Julia started to ask even more questions, and wanted to see her birth certificate, as well as childhood photos. Julia thought that her birth records could have been forged or fraudulent in some way. Their failure to provide sufficient information, left Julia feeling unsatisfied, and she still wanted further proof. She asked her parents to do a DNA test with her, but they both refused.

As a result, Julia started to look through a database

of missing children, and this was how Julia came across the Madeleine McCann case. As Julia looked through some of the e-fits associated with Madeleine's case, she noticed that the e-fit image listed as 4B, had a strong resemblance to her abuser, Peter Ney.

In May 2022, Julia contacted various authorities in the hope that she would receive help whilst seeking answers about her true identity. It was also somewhere around this time, that she was hospitalised after trying to hurt herself again. Despite Julia's concerns, that she could be Madeleine McCann, or another missing child, without carrying out an official DNA test, Operation Grange, amongst other authorities, simply dismissed her claims.

After being rejected by all of these authorities, on February 15, 2023, Julia created an Instagram account, with a profile called @IAmMadeleineMccann. On the account, she stated that she was requesting help, as the UK police, and Polish police were not helping her. Below are the words that was posted on her profile, as well as in her first post.

"I need DNA test. Police investigators from UK and Poland try to ignore me. I will tell my story in posts here. Help me."

"Help me, I need to talk with Kate and Gerry McCann I think I can be Madeleine"

On February 19, 2023, just a few days later, Fia Johansson, a self-proclaimed psychic detective and private investigator, got in touch with Julia, and offered

Seeking Justice

to help her. Julia's account gained a huge amount of interest, and within a small amount of time, the account had over one million followers.

On February 24, 2023 Fia become Julia's official spokesperson, and she openly expressed that it was very strange for Julia's polish parents to refuse to do a DNA test, and was convinced that Julia was trafficked as a child. Fia also claimed that she had been in contact with the McCanns, and that they have agreed to do a DNA test with Julia. It is unclear who first introduced the name Julia Faustyna, or Julia Wendell, instead of Julia Wandelt, but the names were often used by the media.

On March 1, 2023, Fia flew into Poland from Los Angeles, California, to meet with Julia. Although Julia had only known Fia for a short period of time, on March 6, after receiving multiple death threats, Julia agreed to go to the United States with Fia. In the United States, Julia stayed with Fia in her California home, and was treated to several tourist attractions whilst there.

On March 10, 2023, through Radar Online, Fia announced that Julia's DNA samples had been submitted for forensic testing, and that a 23andMe test was being done to establish her ancestry. Somewhere around March 16, Fia gained unauthorised access to Julia's Instagram account, and without permission she changed Julia's password so that she could have full control of Julia's account.

Julia was believed to have been suffering from an unknown illness, and on March 17, 2023, during an online livestream, Fia announced that Julia might have leukaemia. Around two months before the show was discontinued, Fia arranged for Julia to be a guest on the Dr Phil show. The Dr Phil Show was created by Oprah Winfrey, and episode 120 of season 21, "I believe I am Madeleine McCann" was aired to the public on March 27, 2023.

Somewhere around March 31, 2023, Julia called the Orange County police department, and reported that Fia had confiscated her phone and passport, and that she was restricting her movements. The police attended Fia's address, and the situation was somehow resolved.

On April 2, Fia announced that she was given power of attorney over Julia. Fia also claimed that she had accessed over 500 pages of Julia's medical records, and via Radar Online, on February 17, 2009, she said when Julia was only seven years old, she was unresponsive, and was taken to hospital in a coma. According to Fia, Julia was suffering from a rare brain disease, that could have been caused by her being over medicated.

On April 3, 2023, Fia used Radar Online, to reveal that she had received the 23andMe DNA test results. Apparently, the results showed that Julia was 100% Polish, with a tiny percentage being Lithuanian and Russian, however other reports states Lithuanian and Romanian, so it is unclear what result is supposed to be true. Either way, according to Fia, the results proved that Julia is not Madeleine McCann.

The results were shown on Instagram, and despite

Seeking Justice

Fia's earlier statements about Julia being trafficked, she now insisted that the results proved that Dorota, is in fact Julia's biological mother. Fia also announced that Julia would be flying back to Poland to be with her father, as it was now safe for Julia to return.

On April 6, Julia created a post on a new Facebook account. There Julia confirmed that she was back in Poland, but not with her dad. Julia said that Fia was very controlling and explained why she felt the need to call the police on Fia. Julia said Fia made her sign some documents, even though she didn't understand the contents of what she was signing. Julia asked for copies of the documents, but Fia refused, and also would not return her medical records.

On April 17, via Radar Online, Fia claimed that Julia had indecent images of children on her phone, and said the phone had been handed over to the Orange County police department for them to investigate. Julia strongly denied the claims that were made against her, and later confirmed that she was not aware of any police investigations about her, in Poland.

At some point, during a conversation that Julia had with her father, he apparently said to her, that he hopes she doesn't think that they drowned their first child and bought her from the McCanns. Although he may have been joking, that was definitely a very strange comment to make.

Julia's concerns should never have been ignored, and there is no valid reason for refusing to test her DNA

Seeking Justice

in this case. Since 2022, Julia has been trying to seek answers about her true identity. Her reports should have been dealt with by the police, but instead, Julia has now been locked up like a criminal, when all she ever wanted was a simple DNA test, so that she can prove who she really is.

Psalms 37:28; *For the Lord loveth judgment, and forsaketh not his saints; they are preserved for ever: but the seed of the wicked shall be cut off.*

Below is a quotation from one of Julia's previous social media posts:

"Some people think they know me because of what they read about me in social media but at the end, there are only a few people who know me very well. They know I'm a fighter. They know I'm not a liar. They know I'm not crazy. They know what I experienced. They know what I remember. They are the most supportive people that I have ever met. If you don't know me well, you can't judge me. If you weren't in my shoes, you can't judge me."

Seeking Justice

What are her memories?

Deuteronomy 31:6; *Be strong and of a good courage, fear not, nor be afraid of them: for the Lord thy God, he it is that doth go with thee; he will not fail thee, nor forsake thee.*

Although it would be better for you to hear Julia's memories, directly from own mouth, unfortunately there are certain people who are deliberately trying to suppress her story. The information that I am sharing below, has come from the various accounts that she has previously given, and shared.

It is also important to remember, that victims will often recall some of their memories in fragmented parts. Memories can come at different points in time, and can also be triggered by particular events.

In February 2023, when Julia first came to the attention of the public, although she did not remember certain parts of her childhood, she did say her earliest memory was being on a beach with other children, trying to catch the turtles by the ocean. Below is also a quote of one of her posts that she made in 2023 about her earliest memory.

"I don't remember most of my childhood but my earliest memory is very strong and it's about holidays in a hot place where there is a beach and white or very light coloured buildings with apartments. I don't see my family in this memory."

Seeking Justice

According to Julia, she started to receive flashbacks about her childhood memories around October 2023. The order of her memories cannot be confirmed, but I have tried to write them all down in a logical order.

Some of her earlier and happy memories, were of her playing games with other children, such as throwing and catching a ball, and also playing Ring-A-Ring-A-Roses. Adults were also in some of her memories, and Julia has spoken of a particular strong memory, where a blonde-haired woman, was stroking her hair, whilst she was laying down on the bed, and the woman was telling her that she loves her, and that she will find her.

Julia also remembers that she was sexually abused by a man, whilst there were other people in the room, this happened before she was taken. She also remembers being injected with something like a syringe. According to Julia, there were two beds in the room, and she was taken from the bed, that was placed next to a window. She said someone handed her through the window to a thin, and dark-haired male, with tanned skin.

She remembers being carried away, and although she was awake, she was unable to move or speak. The man walked in a diagonal direction, and she remembers looking into the sky, and seeing the full moon. She was taken to a black car, and placed on the back seats, which she described as being grey and black. She was later transferred into some kind of child sized, boxed container. Whilst inside the container, she remembers hearing a woman screaming. She also recalls that the car broke suddenly, but then nothing else after that.

Seeking Justice

She remembers being in underground basements, with grey stone walls, along with other children. Inside these basements, her and the other children, were abused in various ways by masked men. She recalls that one man had a white mask, and another was dressed like a clown. She left the first basement with a man who at the time, called her by a different name. When she left with him, she ended up being on the beach, but no one else was around.

In total, Julia recalls being kept in three different types of underground basements. The third basement contained several child size, grey stone altars, and is where the ritualistic sexual abuse took place. The adults were dressed in black, and whilst abusing children, they were also repeatedly chanting "let us take her, let them take her."

They chose a girl, and she was made to lay down in an X shape. The adults who were stood around her, were wearing some kind of necklace. The adults used something sharp, and then took a small amount of her blood, which they placed into their necklaces.

At one point, Julia remembers that as she was sat on the floor, crying for her mummy and daddy, an adult female came to her and covered her mouth, and she was forced to go somewhere with her.

On one occasion, Julia and another child, who was of a similar age, managed to escape the third basement, for a short period, until they were found. Julia and this child found an exit to the left side of the stone area, which led to a wooden basement, that had a ladder in it. They climbed the ladder, and exited the basement through the high grass that was covering the entrance.

It was very dark outside, and although Julia and the other child were trying to hide, they were caught very quickly by two men. The men took them to the forest, and Julia recalls that one of the men used something sharp to hurt the other child's neck. At the time Julia did not know if the child had survived, as she did not see her again. However, Julia now believes that the child did survive.

In the basements, Julia also remembers two older children, who were somehow attached together, most likely by chains and handcuffs. One of them specifically had a chain around her neck, that was connected to the wall, and restricted her movements. On one of the walls, there were different sized XX's. Some of the abusers who were in the third basement, and participated in the ritualistic abuse, are high profile individuals. As Julia should be the one to officially name them, I have not included their names.

Julia was taken to other places, and recalls that one place had high ceiling with bars on the windows. She remembers being taken to a room that had an oval sign outside with the number 116 on it. She remembers hearing dogs barking, but whilst she was inside this room, Julia was sexually abused, by a man who she knows by name.

Seeking Justice

Julia was also taken on a boat, by a man, who she now recognises. On the boat, he told her that this was the only to help her parents, and that she will need to have a new name. Julia explains that her father had also said something very similar to this before she was taken.

Another memory that Julia spoke about, involved her and an older female child. They were both being chased in the forest, and she was struggling to keep up with the older child, but the older child was still trying to help her. As both children were running, they were actually being hunted and chased by men with spears. The older child got hit by the spear, and then two men separated the girls from each other.

Julia's first memory of her Polish parents, is of her sitting in the back of their car. Her father was driving, and her mother was in the front passenger seat. They drove next to a forest, and she remembers seeing a very small fire, and also a small deer. Julia was upset and wanted to save the deer. She remembers being told that her name is Julia, and she is now their daughter. They spoke with her in English, and said she has to learn Polish. Julia was crying, and whilst the car was still moving, she remembers opening the car door and trying to get out.

Around March 2023, Julia spoke about some of the memories that she had at that time. Most of those memories had been written down in one of her notebooks. I am unsure how old she was at the time of those experiences, but based on the content, I suspect she may have been an older child, or maybe a teenager.

Seeking Justice

Julia has travelled to various luxurious locations, and has memories of riding a camel in the dessert. She has another memory, where she felt panicked and scared, whilst she was locked inside the bathroom with another young girl. She also remembers paragliding with an older male who she didn't know, and because it was not something that she wanted to do, she felt very stressed and scared. She describes the place as luxurious, and recalls seeing camels on the beach.

These are just some of the memories, that Julia was able to share. She has a lot more memories that she did not feel comfortable speaking about. She seems to be protective towards her biological mother, and although she did not elaborate or go into details, she did say that she was also abused by one of her real parents.

This is Julia's account of what she has experienced, and whether you believe her or not, child trafficking still happens. There are multiple survivor testimonies, and detailed documentaries that deal with the facts.

For those who feel that it wouldn't be possible for Julia to recall specific details about her experiences, although she was young, it is important to remember that everyone's brain is different. There are endless amounts of real-life movies, that have demonstrated the amazing skills and abilities of other human beings. Two movies that are definitely worth watching are; 'Believe Me: The Abduction of Lisa McVey', and also 'The Girl Who Escaped: The Kara Robinson Story.'

Seeking Justice

Although Lisa McVey was 17 years old, and Kara Robinson was 15 years old, both girls had the amazing ability to recall fine details, and they are an example, that anything is possible.

Genesis 50:20; *But as for you, ye thought evil against me; but God meant it unto good, to bring to pass, as it is this day, to save much people alive.*

Below is a quotation from one of Julia's previous social media posts:

"No one really understands what I've been through, because it's hard to understand and even harder to explain so that someone understands. It is as if you are trapped even when you are no longer held against your freedom. Free and yet still trapped. Seemingly no longer experiencing violence, but still feeling that it is the only thing you know!"

Seeking Justice

Who should have helped her?

Below, is a list of companies, charities, or departments, that Julia had contacted in 2022, asking for help, due to her concerns that she may be a missing child.

1. *Operation Grange*
2. *Interpol in London*
3. *Scotland Yard (Metropolitan Police Headquarters)*
4. *Crimestoppers*
5. *Leicestershire Police*
6. *Policia Judicaria (National Criminal Police in Portugal)*
7. *Casual Police in Portugal*
8. *Local Police in Poland*
9. *Main Police in Poland (Komenda Główna Policji)*
10. *Polish embassy in UK*
11. *Polish embassy in Portugal*
12. *English embassy in Poland*
13. *English embassy in Portugal*
14. *Ministry of Foreign Affairs in Poland*
15. *A Private Investigator who worked on the McCann case*
16. *X-files team in Poland*
17. *Online campaign: "Find Madeleine"*
18. *Polish consulate in London*
19. *Various Private Detectives from BGP Global Services*
20. *Police in Germany*
21. *Missing People Foundation in UK*
22. *ITAKA Missing People Foundation in Poland*
23. *Fundacja na tropie in Poland*
24. *Church in Praia da Luz, Portugal*

Seeking Justice

The Operation Grange Phone Call

Below is a transcript of the phone call that Julia received from Operation Grange on June 18, 2024. The audio version of this phone call has been shared to the public online, and may still be available on some platforms.

Operation Grange: *How are you?*

Julia: *Who's calling?*

Operation Grange: *It's the police.*

Julia: *Ah okay, police.*

Operation Grange: *I am a Police Officer from The Metropolitan Police.*

Julia: *Okay*

Operation Grange: *And I work on Operation Grange, the Madeleine McCann case.*

Julia: *Okay*

Operation Grange: *And we actually spoke, my name is Mark, we actually spoke a number of years ago.*

Julia: *Yes, twenty twenty-two.*

Seeking Justice

Operation Grange: Yeah, yeah, you rang me when you were in a, in a, in a hospital.

Julia: Yes, I remember you.

Operation Grange: Oh, good, good. So, yeah, so I told you back then that you weren't Madeleine McCann, but obviously, a lot has happened since then. So, I'm just ringing because I'm obviously aware you went to Leicester, to Rothley, at the anniversary, and you also went to Charing Cross Police Station.

Julia: That's true.

Operation Grange: Yeah, and they stated a intelligence report just to say that you attended, and they took your DNA.

Julia: Yes

Operation Grange: So, and then I know that you rang police again on the...

Julia: Yes, because I was worried because no one had called me, and I was like, you know...

Operation Grange: Yeah, yeah, on the thirty-first of May. So obviously, we, we have been following everything, we know everything that's gone on with you, and we, yeah so, we...

Julia: I never lied. I never lied. I mean, everything that was said by this fake fraud, Fia Johansson from USA wasn't true.

Operation Grange: Yeah, well, I mean all I'm going to say is what I said back in, in two thousand and twenty-two. You, you are not Madeleine McCann, okay? I know that's hard to hear. And I know you've been told this by many people, but you have to remember, we, we've worked on this investigation for, since two thousand and eleven, I've worked on this investigation.

Julia: *I know.*

Operation Grange: *Yeah*

Julia: *But, did you get results?*

Operation Grange: *Yeah*

Julia: *Can you give me a copy?*

Operation Grange: *Of what sorry?*

Julia: *Of the DNA results.*

Operation Grange: *Oh, we, we haven't sent the DNA. It's not being tested.*

Julia: *Why?*

Operation Grange: *We can't spend public money on something like that, when there's no, there's no…*

Julia: *Okay, but okay, I don't understand this because, they told me, okay, so why are you, okay can I ask you a question?*

Operation Grange: *Yeah*

Seeking Justice

Julia: *Why are you saying without any testing that I am not Madeleine when I clearly can remember some things because I got flashbacks, and there is a person, there is a person, and listen to me please, don't, don't hang up the phone, there is a person...*

Operation Grange: *No, no, I won't, I'm listening.*

Julia: *Okay, there is a person, who claims, I don't believe in this, but he claims his medium, and I didn't tell anyone about flashbacks that I have, besides on one police, a person from police. I didn't tell anyone, and he knows exactly where I was, and I remember being in basements, and I'm not crazy and you can test me by psychologist, psychiatrist, I had depression. Okay, I had depression, but that is all, and I remember many things, and I don't know how can you say that I'm not Madeleine without any testing.*

Operation Grange: *Okay, so I know the person you talk about, he's a psychic, he's a medium, and we have lots of psychics and mediums contacting us, and there's no, there's no, there's no truth in what they say, okay?*

Julia: *Okay*

Operation Grange: *People have dreams, people are religious, they contact us. We know, we know, that you are not Madeleine McCann, okay? And you're not the first person. I had...*

Julia: *Okay, but, but...*

Operation Grange: *I had an American girl, who had, who had actually, a problem with her eye, and she had thoughts similar* to you. It was very similar. She didn't have, she had some memories when she was a child, etcetera, etcetera, and we had to, and she came, she travelled from the USA to London, and we saw her, and we had to tell her the same thing, that she was not Madeleine.

Julia: *But you got so many funds and you can do the DNA test? Like, I don't understand, like the reason.*

Operation Grange: *Yeah, as I said, as I said, we are happy, we are satisfied, okay, and this is not just me talking, this is the team that work on this investigation. We are happy and satisfied that you are not Madeleine McCann. You are one of many hundreds of people, I'm going to say hundreds, who think they are Madeleine.*

Julia: *But what are you based on? Like there was no DNA test.*

Operation Grange: *I can't go into the details, okay.*

Julia: *Like, but sorry, I mean, with all respect.*

Operation Grange: *It's an ongoing investigation, okay, it's an ongoing investigation. You have, you have had treatment over many years for mental health issues.*

Julia: *Yes, I had, but every single person who would be even abducted would have problem with health.*

Operation Grange: *No, no, what I'm saying is, that unfortunately, unfortunately, having mental health issues is not nice. It's not pleasant.*

Seeking Justice

Julia: *It's not nice, but I'm fine now.*

Operation Grange: *Yeah okay, okay. If you're fine then, you need to accept that you...*

Julia: *But you didn't do DNA tests.*

Operation Grange: *Yeah, but you've got to accept that you've got loving parents and family back home, okay?*

Julia: *What are you talking about!*

Operation Grange: *They are your family, okay? You are not Kate and Gerry's daughter.*

Julia: *But you don't know this because you didn't compare my DNA with them.*

Operation Grange: *I do know from other investigations.*

Julia: *What is the other investigation? You didn't compare DNA.*

Operation Grange: *Like I said, I can't go into details*

Julia: *Okay, but you didn't compare DNA Right?*

Operation Grange: *No, and that's why I'm ringing you. I'm ringing you to tell you that we're not going to compare your DNA, so you don't wait for an answer okay. But you have to accept it, and I understand your reaction, I really do.*

Seeking Justice

Julia: *No, it's not about my reaction. It's about what I can remember. It's about the person who is medium remembers, knows what I remember, and they didn't tell anyone.*

Operation Grange: *Yeah, but I can't, I can't do, there's nothing else I can say, I know that, I know there's nothing else I can say that will change your mind.*

Julia: *No, it's not about changing my mind, it's about fucking DNA. Sorry for my words, but my parents refused to do DNA. You don't want to compare my DNA, and there are many similarities. My abuser looks like a person from picture 4B, so I don't understand. You got, one hundred ninety-two thousand pounds for investigation, and you don't want to compare DNA of someone who says…*

Operation Grange: *It's not about not wanting to okay. We follow, we follow set procedures. It's very hard to explain how investigations work, but we are extremely experienced in this. You are not the first person; You won't be the last person, who says they are Madeleine McCann okay. And we, we understand your reaction, we accept that.*

Julia: *But I'm still saying, you, I mean it's not about the reaction. It's about that you have no proofs against me, like nothing that would say that I am or I'm not, because you didn't check it. And this is, this is unbelievable.*

Operation Grange: *Right, so there's no facts, no facts at all to say you're Madeleine okay.*

Julia: *And no facts that say that I'm not.*

Seeking Justice

Operation Grange: *There's no evidence. So, we go by evidence.*

Julia: *Okay*

Operation Grange: *There is no evidence to say that you're Madeleine. Everything you've said, we have been able to disprove okay.*

Julia: *But you don't know what I remember and you even don't want to know. And what about my abuser?*

Operation Grange: *You've told us before; You've told us before.*

Julia: *No, no, I never tell, listen...*

Operation Grange: *We use our investigation to dispute all the facts.*

Julia: *Okay*

Operation Grange: *Now I've listened to you, I've listened to you, but...*

Julia: *I didn't tell. Please, last thing. Can I say last thing, and then you can do whatever you want, with whatever. I just want to say that I didn't tell about my flashbacks to anyone, and I started getting them since October twenty twenty-three.*

Operation Grange: *Yeah, okay.*

Julia: *So, no one knew.*

Seeking Justice

Operation Grange: *Well, we spoke in twenty twenty-two and I told you, you weren't Madeleine and you accepted that.*

Julia: *No, I never accepted that. I was still trying to...*

Operation Grange: *You did. You did. You did. You did, I made notes, and you said, okay. Now I'm going to finish this call. We're not going to speak to you again, okay. If you ring the police again.*

Julia: *Because you...*

Operation Grange: *Just listen to me, one last thing. We will not speak to you again. If you ring the British police or you go to Leicester again, they will contact, any kind of contact will come back to us, okay. We are Operation Grange. It will come back to us. So, it's pointless you making any more attempts to contact the British police.*

Julia: *Why?*

Operation Grange: *And also, if you do go to Leicester again, and you do, you know, they are fully aware of you now. They know who you are, and if, I mean, there's offenses called harassment here. If you cause any harassment, you could be arrested okay.*

Julia: *Is it blackmail? If I will go there, I will be...*

Operation Grange: *No*

Julia: *Yes, it is blackmail.*

Seeking Justice

Operation Grange: *No, no, harassment is when you annoy someone.*

Julia: *I'm saying that you're blackmailing me now.*

Operation Grange: *No, I'm not blackmailing...*

Julia: *It looks like, it looks like, because I don't harass anyone.*

Operation Grange: *I'm just giving you advice. I'm just giving you advice. Now Julia, I'm really sorry to have to ring you like this. I know you don't...*

Julia: *No, because you just didn't check my DNA, and you admitted this.*

Operation Grange: *Yeah, yeah, and now I need to finish the call, okay.*

Julia: *Okay. I will never give up. This is something that I want to tell you.*

Operation Grange: *I know you won't, okay. But you take care yeah, you take care.*

Julia: *Bye.*

List of Prescribed Medications

Below is a copy of the list of the medications that Julia has previously shared, to show what medications was prescribed between 2010 and 2015. Unfortunately, I can't find the medications for 2015. In 2010, Julia was nine years old, and Madeleine would have been seven years old. As I have previously mentioned, confusion and memory loss were common side effects for these medications.

21.12.2010
Peritol 4mg 1/2 pill per day
Tiapridal 100mg 1 pill per day
Tomapax 15mg 2 pills per day
Elicea 5mg 1 pill per day

Doctor prescribed 3 boxes from every medication:
Tiapridal 1 box x 20 pills, Elicea 2 boxes x 28 pills, Topamax 1 box x 60 pills

25.01.2011
Topamax 50mg 2 pills per day
Tiapridal 100mg 2 pills per day
Escitil 10mg 2 pills per day

Doctor prescribed 3 boxes from every medication:
Tiapridal 3 boxes x 20 pills, Escitil 3 boxes x 28 pills, Topamax 3 boxes x 28 pills

Seeking Justice

18.04.2011
Topamax 50mg 2 pills per day (5 boxes x 28 pills)
Tiapridal 100mg 4 pills per day (46 boxes x 2 pills)
Escitil 10mg 1 pill per day (3 boxes x 28 pills)
Venlectine 37.5mg 1 pill per day (3 boxes x 28 pills)

12.09.2011
Topamax 100mg a few pills per day, I am not sure if I understand it well because he wrote different dose (11 boxes x 28 pills)
Tiapridal 100mg 4 pills per day (4 boxes x 20 pills)
Escitil 10mg 1 pill per day (3 boxes x 28 pills)
Venlectine 37.5mg 1 pill per day (3 boxes x 28 pills)

3.10.2011
Tiapridal 100mg 6 pills per day (6 boxes x 20 pills)

12.12.2011
Topamax 100mg 1 pill per day (4 boxes x 28 pills)
Venlectine 37.5mg 1 pill per day (4 boxes x 28 pills)
Tiapridal 100mg 1 pill per day (16 boxes x 20 pills)
Escitil 10mg 1 pill per day (3 boxes x 28 pills)

12.03.2012
Tiapridal 100mg 4 pills per day (8 boxes x 20 pills)
Toramat 200mg 2 pills per day (4 boxes x 30 pills)
Topamax 100mg 1 pill per day (1 box x 28 pills)
Venlectine 75mg 1 pill per day (3 boxes x 28 pills)

Seeking Justice

10.04.2012
Tiapridal 100mg 4 pills per day (12 boxes x 20 pills)

04.06.2012
Toramat 200mg 2 pills per day (3 boxes x 30 pills)
Tiapridal 100mg 4 pills per day (9 boxes x 20 pills)
Fibraxine 6g 1 per day (6 boxes x 15 pills)
Trilafon 4mg 3 pills per day (1 box x 100 pills)

27.08.2012
Toramat 200mg 2 pills per day (3 boxes x 30 pills)
Trapridal 100mg 4 pills per day (11 boxes x 20 pills)
Valectine 75mg 1 pill per day (3 boxes x 28 pills)
Anafcanil 10mg 1 pill per day (3 boxes x 30 pills)
Tritafon 4mg 3 pills per day (1 box x 100 pills)
Fibraxine 6g 1 per day (6 boxes x 15 pills)

25.10.2012
Tiapridal 100mg 4 pills per day (9 boxes x 20 pills)
Toramat 200mg 2 pills per day (3 boxes x 30 pills)
Trilafon 8mg 2 pills per day (1 box x 100 pills)
Anafranil SR 75mg 1 pill Per day (5 boxes x 20 pills)
Anafranil 25mg 1 pill per day (3 boxes x 30 pills)
Fibraxine 6g 1 pill per day (6 boxes x 15 pills)

Seeking Justice

18.01.2013
Toramat 200mg 2 pills per day (6 boxes x 30 pills)
Tiapridal 100mg 4 pills per day (9 boxes x 10 pills)
Trilafon 8mg 2 pills per day (1 box x 100 pills)
Anafranil SR 75mg 1 pill per day (6 boxes x 20 pills)
Fibraxine 6g 1 per day (6 boxes x 15 pills)

15.03.2013
Tiapridal 100mg 4 pills per day (4 boxes x 20 pills)

19.04.2013
Toramat 200mg 2 pills per day (6 boxes x 30 pills)
Tiapridal 100mg 4pills per day (20 boxes x 20 pills)
Anafranil SR 75mg 1pill per day (12 boxes x 20 pills)
Trilafon 8mg 2 pills per day (2 boxes x 100 pills)
Fibraxine 6g 1 pill per day (6 boxes x 15 pills)

08.07.2013
Anafranil SR 75mg 1 pill per day (6 boxes x 20 pills)
Tiapridal 100 mg 4 pills per day (15 boxes x 20 pills)
Toramat 200 mg 2 pills per day (6 boxes x 30 pills)
Trilafon 8mg 2 pills per day (1 box x 100 pills)
Fibraxine 6g 1 pill per day (6 boxes x 15 pills)

30.09.2013
Tiapridal 100mg 4 pills per day (10 boxes x 20 pills)
Anafranil SR 75mg 1 pill per day (6 boxes x 20 pills)
Toramat 200mg 2 pills per day (6 boxes x 30 pills)
Tisercin 25mg 2 pills per day (2 boxes x 50 pills)

Seeking Justice

13.12.2013
Tiapridal 100mg 4 pills per day (15 boxes x 20 pills)
Toramat 200mg 2 pills per day (6 boxes x 30 pills)
Anafranil SR 75mg 1 pill per day (6 boxes x 20 pills)
Olanzapine Apotex 5mg 1 pill per day
(2 boxes x 28 pills)
Fibraxine 6g. 1 pill per day

03.04.2014
Anafranil SR 75mg 1 pill per day (6 boxes x 20 pills)
Olanzapine Apotex 5mg 1 pill per day
(3 boxes x 28 pills)
Toramat 200mg 2 pills per day (6 boxes x 30 pills)
Tiapridal 100mg 4 pills per day (15 boxes x 20 pills)
Fibraxine 6g 1 pill per day (6 boxes x 15 pills)

The Cover Up Culture

Mark 8:36; *For what shall it profit a man, if he shall gain the whole world, and lose his own soul?*

The disappearance of Madeleine McCann is one of the biggest missing person cases in history. It generated a huge amount of interest all over the world, and as of March 31, 2024, Operation Grange had already spent £13,200,00 on the case. An additional £192,000 was agreed by the Home Office for the 2024-2025 tax year.

If the police believe that Madeleine is dead, then Operation Grange should not receive any more public funding for this case. Some of the people who believe that Madeleine is dead, use the fact that the blood dog, as well as the cadaver dog, both reacted to some kind of scent inside the McCann's apartment.

For arguments sake, let's say that the blood dog was correct, and there was some of Madeleine's blood inside the apartment. However, the reaction of the cadaver dog, is not proof that Madeleine is dead. The apartment was searched, and her body has never been found. I agree that something could have happened within the apartment that caused Madeline to bleed, however, I do not believe that she is dead, or that the reaction of the cadaver dog was correct.

I know of situations first-hand, where alerts by police dogs have been wrong. Although there is usually a good explanation for the dog's reaction, the fact remains that statistically police dogs have been known to make false alerts. It is also possible that the cadaver dog, may also have been reacting to the scent of blood.

Since it cannot be proven that Madeleine is dead, I think it is only fair to consider the fact, that she could still be alive. Therefore, if Madeleine is still alive, Julia's childhood memories, could be extremely relevant in this case. With that in mind, I find it very suspicious, that the police seem to have no interest in speaking to her about these memories.

It is very possible for Julia's abuser Peter Ney, to be a relative of Martin Ney, who was a person of interest in this case. Martin Ney is a convicted serial killer and sex offender, of German heritage. Julia's father has links to Germany, and he is the one who told Julia that Peter Ney was previously involved in kidnappings. These are some serious allegations, that the police should be investigating, so that they can determine whether or not there is a link between the two men.

The police have not provided Julia with any evidence to support their statement that she is not Madeleine McCann. Julia clearly suspects that she may be a kidnapped child, so it is not appropriate for them to merely accept the words of her parents as facts, just because they deny her claim. Do they really think, that if Julia was actually kidnapped, that her parents would admit to their actions, and risk being sent to jail after obtaining their daughter illegally?

Seeking Justice

According to the media, Julia's mother runs a chain of children clothes shops, under the name Coccodrillo, which is the Italian word for crocodile. As you would expect on any website that sells clothes for children, there are many photographs of children on the website. However, I honestly think that some of the images look quite strange.

The text over one of the images reads; 'Small details create big adventures.' What does that even mean? On another image it says; 'Details create great adventures.' They also have a sub heading that says; 'Discover the trends and details hidden in our collections.' Now I fully understand that the site could be totally genuine, but if Julia's mother is involved in child trafficking, then there is actually a risk that the Coccodrillo website could be a front for selling children, as well as clothes.

It should go without saying, that all reports made to the police, will be treated without favour or affection. Nevertheless, it is crystal clear that Julia's reports have not been actioned or taken seriously. We know that it is not easy for victims to come forward, so when they do, it's only right that their claims should be properly investigated and looked into.

Julia is a victim, and since 2023, she has received multiple death threats, for simply claiming that she might be Madeleine McCann. On one occasion she was badly assaulted, and although the incident was reported to the police, no one was ever arrested.

In George Orwell's book; Animal Farm, although

Seeking Justice

the Pigs were once passionate about equality and freedom, but when they got full control, they betrayed and all of their original beliefs, and ended up replacing all previous rules about equality with the follow; "All animals are equal, but some are more equal than others."

The hypocrisy of the Pigs, is no different to the hypocrisy of the police in today's society. Despite all of the extensive training that civil servants and public authorities receive, when it comes down to it, a report from a poor or homeless person, will never be given the same level of respect, as a report from a high-profile individual.

During the phone call, between Julia and Operation Grange, without even asking what her new memories were, Julia was told outright by the officer, that they will not be speaking to her again. She was told that any kind of contact with the British police, would be sent through to themselves, and he made it clear that it is pointless in her making any more attempts to contact the police.

She was advised not to attend Leicester again, and was told that if she did, she could be arrested for Harassment. Although, his statement was quite vague, but for him to suggest that Julia is not allowed to make further contact with the police, or to attend any part of Leicester, is completely unprofessional and unfounded. His suggestion goes against her human rights, and appears to have been a way of scaring her into silence.

We live in a society, where instead of being praised

and supported, whistle-blowers are often victimised and silenced. Julian Assange, the founder of WikiLeaks, was a hacker and an activist, who tried to expose injustice, but ended up being silenced in prison. Throughout history it is evident that cover ups have played a part in many high-profile cases.

The assassination of President John F. Kennedy, took place on November 22, 1963. Although there are still many conspiracies and questions about the case, such as who the real assassin was, there remains a level of cover up on the case. It is believed that many parties were involved in planning the assassination, and this includes official authorities such as, the United States government, the Central Intelligence Agency (CIA) and the Federal Bureau of Investigation (FBI).

Two days after the Presidents assassination, Lee Harvey Oswald was killed. According to the narrative that was being pushed at the time, he was believed to be responsible for the attack. As a way of suppressing the truth, certain testimonies were ignored. Evidence was allegedly tampered with, and witnesses were either intimidated or killed.

Many people always believed that Oswald was part of a much bigger conspiracy, and in 1994, whilst serving a 50-year prison sentence, James Earl Files, openly confessed to being one of the shooters involved in the John F. Kennedy assassination. According to his confession, the government, and many other public officials, were also involved.

Seeking Justice

Today there are many documentaries available, which expose just how governments have been used to mislead and deceive the nations. The practice of withholding information, or even covering up the truth, has been going on for years. However, the time will eventually come, and the truth will always be exposed.

Luke 12:2-3; *For there is nothing covered, that shall not be revealed; neither hid, that shall not be known. Therefore whatsoever ye have spoken in darkness shall be heard in the light; and that which ye have spoken in the ear in closets shall be proclaimed upon the housetops.*

Seeking Justice

Who are they protecting?

1 Timothy 6:10; *For the love of money is the root of all evil: which while some coveted after, they have erred from the faith, and pierced themselves through with many sorrows.*

It is clear that there has been a level of cover up and corruption in the Madeleine McCann case, but the real question is why? Considering that a simple DNA test, would have resolved this situation a long time ago, you have to ask yourself why this was not done?

Julia has the right to know her true identity and if she is a missing child or not. An official DNA test, would prove once and for all, whether or not Julia Wandelt is Madeleine McCann.

Some people think that because Julia had a Polish passport, that means that she lied about never seeing her birth certificate. However, it is also possible that Julia's mother could have applied for a passport on her behalf, when she was a child. If this was the case, then Julia would already have a PESEL number.

A PESEL number is usually assigned to a Polish citizen when a birth is registered. The PESEL number is not displayed on the birth certificate, but it is included on the Polish Identity Card. A child can be issued with an Identity Card, but it is only compulsory if you are 18 years or older, and reside in Poland.

Seeking Justice

The Identity Card can be used instead of a passport to travel to selected countries. We know from Julia's previous accounts that she has visited other countries. In that case, if Julia already had a passport as a child, or even a Polish Identity Card, then it would have been possible for her to renew her passport, without needing to see her birth certificate.

In spite of that, just because Julia has a PESEL number, or a passport, it still does not prove her true identity. It is possible that her PESEL number could have been registered at the birth of another child, whose name would have been Julia Wandelt. If the death of that child was not registered, then it is also possible for that child's identity to have been illegally given to another child.

Even if this was the case, to avoid being caught, the parents are not going to admit that they have used another child to replace a previous child. Just like the family who would have sold or given away their child, would also not admit to their actions. Either way, the scenarios above, are very possible.

Unfortunately, children go missing all the time, but for most cases, they do not receive anywhere near the level of funding or support that the McCann family received. Besides the obvious fact that an abduction could have taken place, the decision to leave three very young children, alone, in an unlocked apartment, that is out sight and out of earshot, shows that the McCanns were unconcerned with the possible risks their children

Seeking Justice

may have experienced whilst they were left alone.

Not only could the children have suddenly become ill, or scared, but there could have been an unexplained emergency within the apartment. These are just a few examples of possible risks, and there have been cases where other parents have been charged for leaving their children alone. Therefore, why is it that the McCanns have not received the same treatment for their actions?

Neglect is a form of child abuse, but for some reason, this couple were able to escape the expected justice. Although the evidence shows that they were guilty of the offence, in this case it was overlooked, probably because of who they know, or are connected to.

Julia's allegations have the potential to ruin the reputation of protected individuals, and because of this, there has been an agenda to silence and discredit her, from the beginning. Why else would the police and authorities have refused to help her back in 2022?

It was because of the continued rejection, why Julia decided to turn to the public. However, within two months of her doing so, her reputation, was completely destroyed. Even though an official DNA test was never carried out, the mainstream media, continue to claim that a DNA test has proven that Julia Wandelt is not Madeleine McCann.

That statement is not true, yet they continue to push out a false narrative. They are repeating the words, of an Independent, Psychic Private Investigator, as if they are facts. It is very possible that the individual in question, could have been paid off to falsify the result. She has no legal association to the official investigation, and Julia Wandelt's DNA, was never compared to the McCanns DNA, or even her Polish mother's DNA.

Why are the mainstream media still intentionally misleading the public? The BBC are also guilty of twisting Julia's words, as they claim that Julia regretted her actions, and apologised to the McCanns. This is also not true, and the only thing that Julia regretted, was the name that she chose for the Instagram account. On reflection, Julia has said, that instead of using the profile name "I am" Madeleine McCann, she now believes it would have been better to call it "am I" Madeleine McCann.

Despite all of the lies, Julia stands firm in her beliefs, and she is still seeking answers about her true identity. There are many people who support Julia, but often, those who attempt to help her, find themselves being threatened or discredited in some way. On more than one occasion, a public petition was set up, to support Julia's request, and her right to have a DNA test. However, without no explanation, each of the petitions were randomly stopped and shut down.

The same is true for those who publicly express anything negative about the McCanns, or their possible involvement in their daughter's disappearance. The careers of some Journalists, who have been brave enough to go against the mainstream narrative, have often been silenced and targeted. The McCanns or their representatives, have also threatened lawsuits, and made certain authors remove their books from popular websites. The McCanns and Goncalo Amaral had a very long legal battle about his book; The Truth of the Lie.

Some people have even tried to reach out to the McCanns, by posting comments on the official Find Madeleine campaign, asking them to do a DNA test with Julia Wandelt, only to find that their comments were removed, and their ability to make further comments, blocked or restricted. If the McCanns had nothing to hide, and were genuinely trying to find their daughter, why would the posts need to be removed?

Even if Kate is convinced that Julia is not Madeleine, based on Julia's accounts, there is a high probability that she could have been trafficked as a child. As an ambassador for charities of missing people, I would have expected Kate to do what she can, to help Julia find out who she is. Nevertheless, rather than helping Julia to get answers, Kate and the rest of her family, ignored Julia's pleas for help. They refused to have a DNA test, and instead, decided to file a police report of Harassment against Julia.

Based on the amount of medication that Julia was given as a child, I strongly believe this was done, to prevent her from remembering things that happened to her. Movies such as Blink Twice, may not be entirely fictitious, and should cause us to think twice, as it gives us a prime example, of how some elites like to spend their time.

Seeking Justice

Some believe that Jill Dando was killed because she wanted to expose a paedophile ring that involved the BBC, and other well-known celebrities such as Jimmy Saville. I don't know if that was true or not, but it is true that the authorities were aware of certain crimes that were being committed by Jimmy Saville, but due to his links and associations, he was allowed to continue with his actions, and get away with his crimes. Too often, we wait for the perpetrator to die, before exposing them to be the monsters that they really are.

In the summer of 2014, two children who lived in Hampstead, North London, claimed that they were abused by their father, and also suggested that their father was a member of a Satanic Paedophile ring. It was claimed that rituals took place in the school ground and also in the local church. The Satanic cult members included parents, Teachers, Social Workers, Police Officers, and Religious Leaders, who were accused of abusing and killing babies, so they could drink their blood.

No other children supported their claims, and the locations or officers named could not be located. There was insufficient evidence to prove that any crimes had taken place, and the children later recanted their claims, by saying that their mother, along with her current partner, had forced them to say it. As a result, the case was dismissed, and closed as a Hoax.

Maybe that was a hoax, but unfortunately, people don't want to admit that there are individuals who

Seeking Justice

participate in satanic and ritual child abuse. Although it didn't focus on ritual abuse, the 'Sound of Freedom' movie was based on real life events, and was able to highlight the fact that children are sometimes trafficked by high-profile individuals. A number of well-known names, have already been exposed for engaging in sexual acts with children, however, there are many more names still to be exposed.

Victims of sexual abuse, are sometimes questioned, in a manner that challenges their memory, rather than one that supports it. Surprisingly, back in 1992, there was actually an organisation called; the False Memory Syndrome Foundation (FMSF). Ironically, it was set up and created by Pamela and Peter Freyd, after their 33-year-old daughter, came forward and accused her father of sexually abusing her when she was a teenager.

Her parents rejected the allegations, and blamed the fabrications on their daughter's therapist, who she was seeing for her panic attacks. The organisation was made to support and advocate for individuals who had been falsely accused of child abuse. Apparently, they wanted to prove that it was possible for victims to create false memories, based on their inner thoughts and fantasies. Thankfully, the company was closed in 2019, but for victims to distinguish between true and false memories, they attempted to suppress the truth, by making their victims doubt their memories.

It is no longer classified information that in the United States, the CIA, carried out secret manipulation and human experiments, on many individuals without their knowledge or consent. The experimental project was known as MK Ultra, and it took place between 1953 and 1973. The project was revealed to the public in 1975, but most of the records about the experiments were already destroyed.

As part of the Mind Control research, the MK Ultra project used LSD, or other drugs, on its candidates without their knowledge or consent. The experiments included brainwashing and psychological techniques, and one of their goals was to wipe clean the minds of their subjects, so that they could then program them as a robot agent. The MK Ultra experiments were a clear violation of an individual's Human Rights.

Throughout the experiments, several participants mysteriously died, whilst others reportedly took their own life during the experiments. Although it is alleged that the MK Ultra project was stopped in 1973, it is still possible, for these types of unethical experiments to happen without us knowing.

When 'Three Identical Triplets' was aired in 2018, it revealed that a New York agency, had deliberately separated the triplets at birth, as part of an experiment. Although this experiment would have been on a much smaller scale compared to MK Ultra, it was revealed that an undisclosed number of twins, had also been separated at birth, as part of the experiment.

For all we know, Madeleine McCann could actually be part of a secret experiment. Perhaps someone has tried to wipe her brain, and reprogram her under a new identity. Although this is just a theory, considering the society that we live in, it is possible that someone might want to do such a thing.

Although it may be possible to cause temporary memory loss, deep inside the body never forgets, and the hidden trauma will eventually resurface. Despite the attempts of scientists, they will never fully be able to control an individual.

Ephesians 6:12; *For we wrestle not against flesh and blood, but against principalities, against powers, against the rulers of the darkness of this world, against spiritual wickedness in high places.*

Who is telling the truth?

Proverbs 3:5-6; *Trust in the Lord with all thine heart; and lean not unto thine own understanding. In all thy ways acknowledge him, and he shall direct thy paths.*

Below, is a brief summary of the accounts that have been given, by different people who are associated with this case in some way. I have also added my own theory for you to see.

The McCann Parents

From the very beginning, the McCann parents have stuck to their original claim, which is that Madeleine was abducted from her bed, by an unknown predator. They do not blame themselves for what happened to Madeleine, and say the guilt should lie with whoever took Madeleine from her bed.

They strongly deny playing any role in Madeleines disappearance, and have expressed how important it is that they find their daughter. Although they are aware that Madeleine may still be alive, and somewhere out there, it appears that they have chosen not to register their DNA with any online website, and they also seem to be very selective about who they are actually willing to do a DNA test with.

Seeking Justice

Nevertheless, a demonstration of their love, can be seen in the fact, that only 12 days after their daughter was said to have been taken, one of their priorities was set up and register a limited business, in her honour, called; Madeleine's Fund: Leaving no stone unturned. Despite the companies name, in the ongoing search for Madeleine, it appears as though the McCanns have left some stones unturned.

Allegedly, the main aim of the business, was to help the family find and locate Madeleine McCann, but any funds received, could in fact be spent to support the McCanns in any way that they deemed fit. At one point, they decided to spend some of the money that had been kindly donated to them, on their mortgage. Although some of the money was used on private investigators, a large portion of the money, was also spent on their legal fees, in the case that they filed against Goncalo Amaral, after he released a book, that accused them of lying and being deceptive.

More recently, the McCanns have come under serious alarm and distress from Julia, and as a result they reported her behaviour to the police. According to Julia, she has been trying to get in touch with the McCanns, so that they could do a DNA test with her, but according to the McCanns, although Julia resides in Poland, she has apparently been stalking and harassing the McCanns for around a year, and as a result of her behaviour, she has caused their family, huge alarm and distress.

Seeking Justice

The Polish Parents

According to Julia's Polish parents, Julia is their biological Daughter. However, despite Julia's multiple requests, they refuse to do a DNA test with her and are unwilling to provide the evidence that would show if their claim is true. It's understandable why they would have initially denied the request, but at some point, it should have become apparent to them, that the not knowing, is actually having a negative effect, on their daughter's mental health and wellbeing.

Nevertheless, they decided that it would probably be better to let Julia's concerns fester for a number of years, in the hope that she would eventually move on. They clearly have not given any consideration to the fact that Julia's child abuse could have caused her to develop trust issues within the family circle.

Although they describe Julia as being someone who suffers with mental health issues, they believe that they have handled the situation well, and that there is no need for them to do a DNA test. Instead, they verbally insist that they are Julia's birth parents, and basically expect Julia to accept their word as truth.

It doesn't matter that a DNA test would actually resolve the matter once and for all, out of principle they are clearly not ready to put this issue to bed. At some point, they apparently stopped having contact with Julia, due to her lies and manipulation. When they heard that Julia was arrested in the UK for harassing the McCanns, instead of reconsidering whether or not they should do the DNA test, according to an online report, Julia's mother and her stepfather were distressed and at their wits end, apparently because of all of the public attention, so they fled their home and went into hiding.

The Police Investigators

Police forces in various parts of the world, have played a part in searching for Madeleine McCann. Despite all these searches, Madeleine has never been found, and although some investigators do believe that Madeleine is dead, her remains have never been found, and there is no evidence to fully support that theory.

If the police have received a third-party report from a convicted criminal, about the possible involvement of another criminal, that is known as hearsay, and is not evidence. If the police had any evidence to prove that their prime suspect, Christian B, was involved in any way in this case, then he should have been charged by now. Instead, it seems as if they are using him, as some kind of scapegoat.

Tunnel vision can lead officers down the wrong path, and perhaps this is what has prevented them from looking into all of the relevant leads. When the case was taken over by Operation Grange, they were quick to announce that the McCann parents were not suspects.

However, for any investigation to be done properly, you have to start from the very beginning. This means, that the parents should have been classed as suspects, until it can be conclusively proven otherwise. There is no concrete evidence to prove that Madeleine is dead, and there is also no concrete evidence to prove that her parents were not involved in her disappearance.

The role of the police should be to determine the facts, by conducting a thorough investigation. If there is a chance that Madeleine is still alive, then it is their responsibility to get to the truth. Their refusal to do a DNA test is very concerning, and also very suspicious.

Goncalo Amaral

Goncalo Amaral was the lead detective in the Portuguese investigation into the disappearance of Madeleine McCann. Goncalo Amaral was removed from the case in October 2007, and in 2008 he released a book about his views of the investigation, called; The Truth of the Lie. He firmly believes that Madeleine was accidentally killed by her parents, and that they used the abduction theory to cover up their crime.

He believes that the McCanns and their friends were deceptive, and claims that they provided no evidence to prove that an abduction had taken place. Although part of his analysis may be true, there is also no concrete evidence to prove that Madeleine is dead. The reaction of the dogs to something in the McCanns apartment, is not evidence that Madeleine is dead.

Seeking Justice

Fia Johansson

Fia Johansson, is allegedly a doctor, as well as an entrepreneur who was born in Iran, but raised in Sweden. She has a Master's Degree in Psychology, and professionally she is known as the Persian Medium, Psychic Detective. She has an impressive profile, which includes being a licensed Private Investigator, a Film Producer, an Actress, an Author, and a Life Coach.

In February 2023, when Fia first started to help Julia with her case, she was supportive of Julia, and very open in her belief that Julia was a trafficked child, and not the child of her Polish parents. Fia publicly condemned Julia's polish parents for refusing to do a DNA test with her, and claimed that she would arrange for a DNA test to be carried out between Julia and the McCanns.

After knowing her for only 15 days, Fia persuaded Julia to go with her to the United States. Fia had a lot of positive things to say about Julia to begin with, but things slowly went downhill. After taking control of Julia's social media account, Fia also became Julia's official Power of Attorney. It is hard to know whether Fia had Julia's best interest at heart, or whether she just liked the power of being in control.

Julia reported Fia to the police, because Fia was withholding her phone and passport from her. This only happened a few days before the DNA test results were released, so it's very hard to know for sure, whether or not someone paid Fia to tamper with the swabs, or compromised the results in any way.

Seeking Justice

Fia claims that Julia's ancestry results, prove that Julia is 100% Polish, and therefore not Madeleine McCann. However, without being able to compare Julia's results to any other family member, the results are still very questionable. Fia, had stated very clearly, that there was sufficient evidence to prove that Julia had definitely been trafficked to Poland.

Then all of a sudden, Fia changes her mind, and says the results prove that Julia's Polish mother is her biological mother. Fia has also accused Julia of being a con-artist, and of being involved in a paedophile ring. Her drastic change of view, makes you wonder if she could have been paid to change her mind.

Is it just a coincidence that Jeffrey Epstein was one of the investors associated with Radar Online? They were the source that Fia used to release any exclusive information about Julia. Was Fia an opportunist in this situation, who was merely seeking fame and attention?

The Mainstream Media

According to the narrative in the mainstream media, the McCann parents are victims, who have played no part in their daughter's abduction. However, when it comes to Julia, she is nearly always described as a delusional fantasist, who is refusing to accept the truth. The mainstream media continue to push the narrative that Julia is a fake, because a DNA test has already proven that she is not Madeleine.

There are also reports that claim Julia acknowledged her mistakes, and apologised for hurting the McCann family. They also support the claims of Julia's Polish parents, and present Julia as being someone who is struggling with mental health issues.

After Julia's arrest, there were several reports, which again used words such as fake, delusional, and fantasist, to describe Julia. Julia is portrayed as an individual whose behaviour is apparently affecting the lives of others. However, there is never any regard for how Julia's life has been affected by the false information that has been shared about her.

Eugenea Collins

Eugenea was born on October 23, 2002, and lives in the United States. Ironically, she first seems to have showed up online, just a few days after Julia's arrest. Although the timing is quite suspicious, Eugenea claims that it was after seeing Julia Wandelt on the Dr Phil show in 2023, that she was drawn in by the images, and began to believe that she is Madeleine McCann.

Eugenea was adopted as a child, and claims that she has never seen her original birth certificate, and that the certificate that she had seen, had someone else's name crossed out on it. As a result of her name not matching official documents, Eugenea says that she has been unable to obtain any official identification. Her social media profiles, includes photos of herself, that have been compared to Madeleine.

With a similar claim to Julia, Eugenea said her local police force has not taken her reports seriously, and she claims that she has unsuccessfully, been trying to get hold of Operation Grange since 2024. Eugenea also alleges that when she saw a photo of Christian B, the prime suspect in the Madeleine McCann case, she instantly recognised him as the man who she had previously been told was her biological father.

Julia Wandelt

For years, Julia has doubted whether her Polish parents were her biological parents or not. They insist that she was not adopted, and although they claim to be her birth parents, they refuse to put her mind at ease by doing a DNA test to prove that what they are saying is true.

As Julia's doubts and concerns grew over time, she eventually reached out to various organisations for help. Although many of these organisations have a duty of care towards victims, nobody was willing to help her. Instead, she was pushed away and rejected, and without any concrete evidence, she was expected to accept and believe the claims of her Polish parents.

When Julia took to social media, she gained a huge amount of public interest, and within a short period of time, Fia Johansson began controlling the information that was being shared to the public. Initially Fia seemed to have Julia's best interest at heart, and said that she is trying to help Julia get to the truth. After a very short period of partnership, Julia ended up reporting Fia to the police, claiming that Fia had been restricting her liberty. Ever since then, the relationship between Fia and Julia has been negative.

Nevertheless, Julia remained firm in her belief, and continued to seek answers. In October 2023, Julia started having flashbacks from her childhood. Despite her flashbacks, the authorities continued to reject her, and have no interest in hearing about any of her memories. Due to the continued rejection, in 2024, Julia started to speak about her memories online.

Slowly, more and more people were becoming aware of Julia's side of the story. At first, people were under the impression that an official DNA test had already been done, so when they realised that it wasn't, they were surprised. Just as the truth was beginning to be revealed, it appears that attempts have been made to silence Julia and prevent her truth from coming out.

<u>My Personal Opinion</u>

We are all entitled to our own opinions, and I want to share my opinion, of what I think has happened to Madeleine McCann. I believe that the McCann's know who Julia is, but they have been lying to the public, so that they don't get caught. I believe they willingly sold their daughter, and the abduction was planned as a way of them covering their tracks, and getting away with

Seeking Justice

their actions.

Madeleine was taken underground, probably for a few days, and although she was still very young, whilst there, she experienced unimaginable sexual and ritual abuse. Some of the adults who took part in these practices, are well-respected individuals who are known by the public.

After a brief period underground, Madeleine ended up with her new family, and lived under a new name. In my opinion, her new family lost their first daughter, either accidentally, or via some sort of sacrifice. As a replacement for their original daughter, they raised Madeleine under the identity of their deceased child. As Madeleine was still a young child, she got used to her new identity, and as expected, she learnt the language appropriate for where she was now living.

Whilst in the care of her new parents, Madeleine, whose new name was now Julia, suffered further sexual abuse. Not only was she abused by a family member, but I believe, that she was probably rented out by her mother to various elite members of secret societies.

Due to the treatment that Julia received, I believe her childhood memories were intentionally suppressed through the use of multiple medications, which were known for their ability to cause memory loss. As a result of being prescribed these medications for a long period of time, Julia was able to forget about her true identity.

Although Julia eventually became suspicious of her

new parents, when she reached out to authorities for help, unfortunately she was rejected. In my opinion, many of the officers working on Operation Grange, along with several government officials, already knew that Julia Wandelt, was the real Madeleine McCann.

However, in order to stop the members of their secret societies from going to jail, they have deliberately covered up the truth. The mainstream media are also complicit in this cover up, and they are intentionally being used to discredit and tarnish Julia's reputation.

Who do you believe?

In relation to the Madeleine McCann case, there are a lot theories out there, so it is hard for people to decide who is telling the truth. For some people, the goal is to conceal the truth, rather than reveal the truth.

Considering how much evidence is available in the public domain, if you search hard enough, you should at least be able to get to some of the truth. Whatever way you look at it, Madeleine was an innocent child, whose life has been affected by all of this. Regardless of the many different opinions about this case, I hope that one day the truth will be revealed to us all!

Ecclesiastes 3:17; *I said in mine heart, God shall judge the righteous and the wicked: for there is a time there for every purpose and for every work.*

Final Conclusion

Psalms 27:1; *The Lord is my light and my salvation; whom shall I fear? the Lord is the strength of my life; of whom shall I be afraid?*

On August 4, 2008, the files and documents from the original Portuguese investigations were made available to the public via; http://www.mccannpjfiles.co.uk

The Policia Judiciaria in Portugal investigated the disappearance of Madeleine McCann between May 4, 2007 and July 21, 2008. Some of the contents within these files are very interesting, and eye-opening. It is also within these files that Julia has been able to access what is believed to be Madeleine's DNA profile.

It takes a lot of courage for victims to come forward and report to the police what has happened to them. For certain crimes, victims are nearly always believed, but for some crimes, victims are inappropriately questioned, and treated as if they are not telling the truth. Unless, there is evidence to prove that a victim is lying, it is important for victims to be believed and treated with respect.

It is very common for victims of sexual abuse to experience mental health issues, and many of the victims who have experienced this type of abuse, have been known to attempt suicide. By not taking Julia's

Seeking Justice

report seriously, she has been deprived of the necessary support and advice that she should have received, as a victim of crime.

When you listen to the voice recording of the phone call that Julia had with Operation Grange, it is very clear by the tone of the officer who spoke to her, that he used her Mental Health, as a reason to dismiss and disregard her claims. He claims that it would not be appropriate for Operation Grange to spend public money on a DNA test.

If a DNA test is not an appropriate way of spending public money, it makes you wonder what £13,200,000 worth of public money has actually been spent on. Not only is a DNA test inexpensive, but it is also the only way to conclusively prove whether or not Julia Wandelt is Madeleine McCann.

If Operation Grange have evidence to prove that Julia is not Madeleine, why are they unable to provide her with this evidence? The Officer assured Julia that she has 'loving parents, but without doing a DNA test, how do they know that they are her biological parents? It's obvious that their actions do not match up with the actions of loving parents.

A loving and biological parent, would have avoided this whole situation, by agreeing to do a DNA test, as the results would prove that they have been telling the truth all along. Considering that Julia has been arrested, where are those loving parents now?

Seeking Justice

After her arrest, it was reported in various online articles that Julia's Polish parents were forced to flee their home and go into hiding for their own safety. Perhaps Julia was getting too close to the truth, so they decided to flee, to avoid being forced to prove that they are Julia's parents, and that she was not obtained in an illegal way.

Also, whilst on the topic of loving parents, isn't it logical for the loving parents of a child who has been kidnapped, to want to do a DNA test with someone who believes that they could potentially be their long-lost daughter.

As of March 31, 2024, the balance in the Madeleine: Leaving No Stone Unturned Fund was just over one million pounds. This is more than enough money to cover a simple DNA test, and if no stone is to be left unturned, why is a DNA test not being done? If the McCanns are genuinely looking for their daughter, and have nothing to hide, then there is no reason for them not to do the test.

At one time, Kate and Gerry professed that they would do anything to find Madeleine. However, it appears that doing a DNA test with Julia, is not something they wish to do. Despite Julia's beliefs, and her attempts to make contact with the McCann's, they refuse to even engage with Julia.

Kate and Gerry, would usually attend the vigil that was being held annually in remembrance of Madeleine McCann. However, in May 2024, Kate and Gerry, along with their twins, were all absent from the event. Instead of showing up, it was reported that they opted to utilise the bank holiday weekend, to take a well-deserved, break away. The location of the break was not disclosed, and it is unknown if the twins also attended the break away.

Despite none of the immediate family being in attendance, the McCann's left a pre-planned message for the guests, which was read out by the Reverend. In their message, they apologised for their absence, and thanked those who attended.

Other than the two years where the event was affected by Covid restrictions, the vigil has taken place every year, since Madeleine went missing. I suppose it was just a coincidence, that the first time Julia Wandelt attends the vigil, that's the first time that an immediate member of the McCann family happens to be absent.

According to the mainstream media, Julia is often described as a "faker" but if Julia was really a fake, then why would she pursue the McCanns for a DNA test? If she was fake, and the McCanns agreed to do the test, then the results would prove that she is not Madeleine, and that she is in fact, a crazy liar, and a fake.

On the other hand, if the McCann's agreed to do a DNA test, and the results proved that Julia was telling the truth, and was in fact the real Madeleine McCann, it would also prove that there has been a level of cover up in this case. Whichever way you look at it, a DNA test needs to be done.

Seeking Justice

With the level of deception and corruption that has already been displayed, it is hard to believe that Julia will have a fair trial. Even if the authorities suddenly agreed to do a DNA test, you really have to wonder how authentic the test results would be. In my opinion, any tests conducted for this case, will need to be publicly sealed, and then independently tested and verified by multiple agencies.

Julia has been seeking answers for a long time, and she has the right to know her true identity. Regardless of whether you believe her or not, she deserves answers. It's because the authorities are desperate for her to remain silent, that they refuse to do the test. If Julia was a delusional fantasist, wouldn't a DNA test still be the best way to resolve this? If they have nothing to hide, then surely there is still more to gain, than there is to lose, by doing the test.

Hebrews 11:1; *Now faith is the substance of things hoped for, the evidence of things not seen.*

On February 17, 2025, only two days before her arrest, Julia posted the following on her Facebook account:

*"I want to say **THANK YOU** to all of my supporters and people who are currently helping me to get the full truth. I would never be able to be in a place where I am now without your help. Do you know what is the best in this journey for the truth and justice?*

Seeking Justice

You are the best. You are the best people I've met in my life so far. You, your support and your kindness. I have never experienced this kind of love and care from anyone in my life. I am very grateful for having you in my life. You are the most visible evidence and example of how people can unite to fight for the truth and justice.

I hope that I will fully find out the truth and that I will get justice. I do not think that I ask for a lot. Simple official DNA test can solve it one way or another. Silence of Kate & Gerry McCann, the police and my polish parents...it speaks volumes.
Thank you for your support"

Uplifting Bible Verses

I hope that the one true God, will continue to protect Julia and keep her safe throughout this difficult time. She has already been through so much, and although there may be times when she feels week, I will pray for her continued strength, and I hope that she will never lose faith.

Psalms 23
The Lord is my shepherd; I shall not want.
He maketh me to lie down in green pastures: he leadeth me beside the still waters.
He restoreth my soul: he leadeth me in the paths of righteousness for his name's sake.
Yea, though I walk through the valley of the shadow of death, I will fear no evil: for thou art with me; thy rod and thy staff they comfort me.
Thou preparest a table before me in the presence of mine enemies: thou anointest my head with oil; my cup runneth over.
Surely goodness and mercy shall follow me all the days of my life: and I will dwell in the house of the Lord for ever.

Psalms 25:5; *Lead me in thy truth, and teach me: for thou art the God of my salvation; on thee do I wait all the day.*

Psalms 31:24; *Be of good courage, and he shall strengthen your heart, all ye that hope in the Lord.*

Seeking Justice

Psalms 33:22; *Let thy mercy, O Lord, be upon us, according as we hope in thee.*

Psalms 37:8-9; *Cease from anger, and forsake wrath: fret not thyself in any wise to do evil. For evildoers shall be cut off: but those that wait upon the Lord, they shall inherit the earth.*

Psalms 62:7; *In God is my salvation and my glory: the rock of my strength, and my refuge, is in God.*

Psalms 121
I will lift up mine eyes unto the hills, from whence cometh my help.
My help cometh from the Lord, which made heaven and earth.
He will not suffer thy foot to be moved: he that keepeth thee will not slumber.
Behold, he that keepeth Israel shall neither slumber nor sleep.
The Lord is thy keeper: the Lord is thy shade upon thy right hand.
The sun shall not smite thee by day, nor the moon by night.
The Lord shall preserve thee from all evil: he shall preserve thy soul.
The Lord shall preserve thy going out and thy coming in from this time forth, and even for evermore.

Psalms 119:114; *Thou art my hiding place and my shield: I hope in thy word.*

Psalms 130:5; *I wait for the Lord, my soul doth wait, and in his word do I hope.*

Seeking Justice

Psalms 140:12; *I know that the Lord will maintain the cause of the afflicted, and the right of the poor.*

Proverbs 21:15; *It is joy to the just to do judgment: but destruction shall be to the workers of iniquity.*

Isaiah 40:31; *But they that wait upon the Lord shall renew their strength; they shall mount up with wings as eagles; they shall run, and not be weary; and they shall walk, and not faint.*

Isaiah 41:10; *Fear thou not; for I am with thee: be not dismayed; for I am thy God: I will strengthen thee; yea, I will help thee; yea, I will uphold thee with the right hand of my righteousness.*

Jeremiah 17:7; *Blessed is the man that trusteth in the Lord, and whose hope the Lord is.*

Lamentations 3:22-26;
It is of the Lord's mercies that we are not consumed, because his compassions fail not. They are new every morning: great is thy faithfulness. The Lord is my portion, saith my soul; therefore will I hope in him. The Lord is good unto them that wait for him, to the soul that seeketh him. It is good that a man should both hope and quietly wait for the salvation of the Lord.

Seeking Justice

Hosea 12:6; *Therefore turn thou to thy God: keep mercy and judgment and wait on thy God continually.*

Zephaniah 3:17; *The Lord thy God in the midst of thee is mighty; he will save, he will rejoice over thee with joy; he will rest in his love, he will joy over thee with singing.*

Zechariah 7:9; *Thus speaketh the Lord of hosts, saying, Execute true judgment, and shew mercy and compassions every man to his brother.*

Romans 15:13; *Now the God of hope fill you with all joy and peace in believing, that ye may abound in hope, through the power of the Holy Ghost.*

Romans 8:24; *For we are saved by hope: but hope that is seen is not hope: for what a man seeth, why doth he yet hope for?*

1 Corinthians 13:13; *And now abideth faith, hope, charity, these three; but the greatest of these is charity.*

Hebrews 10:30; *For we know him that hath said, Vengeance belongeth unto me, I will recompense, saith the Lord. And again, The Lord shall judge his people.*

Printed in Dunstable, United Kingdom

70221863R00050